CHRISTMAS
COLORING BOOK FOR KIDS

ILLUSTRATIONS BY:

DREAM. INSPIRE. CREATE.

VISIT US ONLINE:
www.youngdreamerspress.com

TAG US IN YOUR PHOTOS & VIDEOS:
www.instagram.com/youngdreamerspress
www.tiktok.com/@youngdreamerspress

WE'RE ALSO ON FACEBOOK:
www.facebook.com/youngdreamerspress

ISBN-13: 978-1-777375-33-1

BUT WAIT, THERE'S MORE!

VISIT GO.YOUNGDREAMERSPRESS.COM/CHRISTMAS

To join our newsletter and
make their world more colorful with
free printable coloring pages!

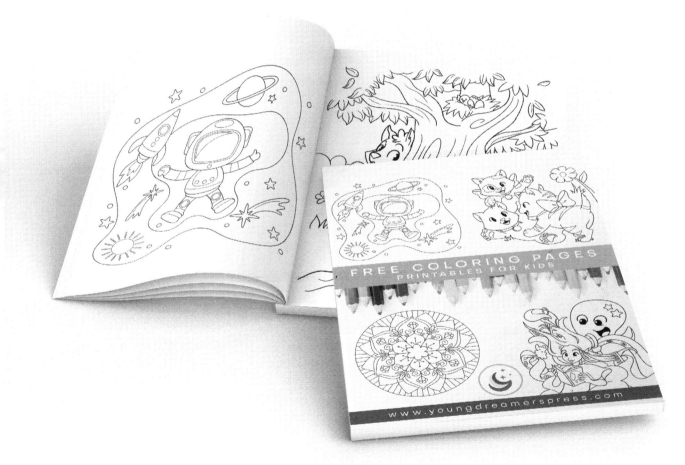

All pages sized for 8.5 x 11 paper and include a wide range of subjects including:
animals, kittens, mermaids, unicorns, mandalas, an astronaut, planets,
a firetruck, a construction vehicle, cupcakes, and more!

978-1-989387-13-9

978-1-989387-46-7

978-1-989387-94-8

978-1-989387-96-2

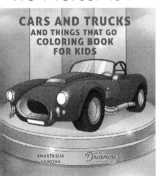

978-1-989790-09-0

978-1-989790-13-7

978-1-989790-41-0

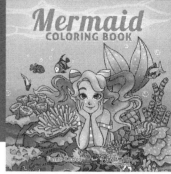

978-1-989790-64-9

978-1-989387-87-0

978-1-989387-88-7

978-1-777375-33-1

978-1-990136-03-0

978-1-989790-93-9

978-1-989790-95-3

978-1-777375-31-7

978-1-777375-32-4

Made in the USA
Las Vegas, NV
10 December 2021

36983741R00037